TEEN GUIDE

JOB SEARCH

TEEN GUIDE

JOB SEARCH

10 EASY STEPS TO YOUR FUTURE

Donald L. Wilkes

Viola Hamilton-Wilkes

TEEN GUIDE JOB SEARCH
10 EASY STEPS TO YOUR FUTURE

iUniverse books may be ordered through booksellers or by contacting:

iUniverse
1663 Liberty Drive
Bloomington, IN 47403
www.iuniverse.com
1-800-Authors (1-800-288-4677)

Because of the dynamic nature of the Internet, any web addresses or links contained in this book may have changed since publication and may no longer be valid. The views expressed in this work are solely those of the author and do not necessarily reflect the views of the publisher, and the publisher hereby disclaims any responsibility for them.

Any people depicted in stock imagery provided by Thinkstock are models, and such images are being used for illustrative purposes only.
Certain stock imagery © Thinkstock.

ISBN: 978-0-5953-9696-2 (sc)
ISBN: 978-0-5958-4102-8 (e)

Print information available on the last page.

iUniverse rev. date: 01/28/2020

First reprint 1991
Second reprint 1992
Third reprint 1993
Fourth reprint 2004
Fifth reprint 2006
Six reprint 2013
Seventh reprint 2020

Published by JEM/Job Educational Materials 1989-1993

Published by WSE/Wilkes Solutions Enterprises 2004

ISBN:0-9628787-1-5

Library of Congress Catalog Card Number: 91-090812

Attention schools, bookstores, libraries, and teachers: Quantity discounts and special purchase arrangements are available. For more information, contact:

Donald & Viola Wilkes

E-mail: <u>teenguide@roadrunner.com</u>

This book is dedicated to the memory of Freda Hamilton.
She touched the lives of so many people in very special ways.
Her light still shines.

Words from the Authors

This job search manual will be an important step toward helping young people find their places in society.

We would like to give special thanks to the following individuals for their invaluable assistance in the completion of our easy-to-read manual: Takiyah A. Wilkes, Steven A. Fuller, Carl Carter, Dorothy Gardner, Judy Larson, Ray Clark, Stefanie Rico, Pamela Simon, and Anne Duffy.

About the Authors ✳

Donald L. Wilkes: Donald is an excellent communicator with years of experience as a job search trainer. He has hired and trained in private industry for companies ranging from small businesses to national retail chains. Donald has also worked with summer youth programs, and enjoys helping young people reach their goals.

Viola Hamilton-Wilkes: Viola has a passion for people and is a terrific communicator. She has a broad interviewing and managing background. Additionally, Viola specializes in training and motivating young people. She also loves to mentor and coach individuals to excel beyond their dreams.

Contents

Introduction

Why do you go to school?

You can bet that answers to this question will not always be the same. Many students would say, "I go to school because my parents make me!" Most parents and teachers would give reasons like "you need an education to be successful," or "school will help you to become a good citizen and be somebody." Some would even say, "because we want our children to be the smartest in the world!" To be honest with you, each of these statements has some truth.

However, the most important reason you go to school is to get an education and a good job!

In many of our schools, young people are learning that they need a job, but are not being taught how to get one.

To get you ready for your job search, we have written an easy-to-read step-by-step guide. This book will cover everything you need to know before you look for a job, and many of the things you need to know once you start working.

Looking for a job may scare you a little. As with most things in life, though, your fear will disappear once you know what you are doing. After you study this guide, your job hunting will be a lot easier.

Let's get started!

Step 1: → Know What You Like and Dislike

Before you look for a job, you should ask yourself some questions that will help you decide what kind of work you want. Since a lot of people spend most of their lives working, it is a good idea to search for a job that you will like. Usually, people who enjoy their jobs do better work than people who don't.

Asking yourself the following questions will help you discover what kind of job will be best for you.

- What subjects do you like in school?

- Are there subjects you've never studied, but find interesting?

- Do you like being around people?

- Do you like being alone?

- Do you like working with older people, including senior citizens?

- Do you like working with children?

- Do you like working with animals?

- Do you like working outside?

- Do you like computers?

- Do you already have some specific job skills (for example, typing or running a cash register)?

- What activities do you enjoy outside of school?

Now that these questions have you thinking about what you like, try asking your working friends, relatives, and even some teachers what they like about their jobs. A few will tell you that they wish they had considered their likes and dislikes before they got their first job or the job they have now. They can tell you that thinking about these questions before looking for a job will put you way ahead in your job search. Remember that your answers to these questions may change as you grow older. What's important is that you keep these ideas in mind.

You should remember one thing:

You will spend most of your life working different jobs, so why not spend that time doing jobs you like? When you love what you do, it does not feel like work!

TIP: Take time to think about the things you enjoy doing. Then find out if you can find that type of work, because it is great to love your job!

Step 1 → Review

1. John is good at sports. His best subjects are English, math, and social studies. John is popular at school, very outgoing, and friendly with people. He has also been chosen as "best dressed" in his class.

    Based on this information, choose the job that you think John would like best.

    a. Pizza delivery person

    b. Stockroom helper

    c. Department store salesperson

    d. Gardener

---

2. Kelly loves animals. She has a pet hamster, a dog, and goldfish. Her favorite subjects in school include music, biology, computers, and typing. Kelly is a friendly person, but she is shy. She likes to wear jeans and tennis shoes most of the time.

    Based on this information, choose the job that you think Kelly would like best.

    a. Restaurant cook

    b. Doctor's office receptionist

    c. Veterinary assistant

    d. Computer salesperson

---

3. Pat is good at sports and likes kids. He learned to swim when he was only five years old. He enjoys going camping with his family and has belonged to a local camping club for three years.

    Based on this information, choose the job that you think Pat would like best.

    a. Pizza delivery person

    b. Tour guide at Disneyland

    c. Cashier

    d. Summer camp counselor

---

4. Kim grew up in the city. She loves to read. At her home, she has at least twenty nonschool related books. People tell her that she is smart, and she likes to share what she learns.

    Based on this information, choose the job that you think Kim would like best.

    a. Book store clerk

    b. Shoe store clerk

    c. Waitress

    d. Tutor

Step 1 → Answers

1. Answer = c

   A salesperson needs to be friendly and nice to customers. A salesperson must dress in a professional manner; for example, John would wear a dress shirt, tie, slacks, and dress shoes. Salespeople work with money and need to have a good understanding of simple math.

   This job requires an employee who likes the same things as John; therefore, it's a job that John probably would like doing.

2. Answer = c

   Anyone who works at a veterinary clinic needs to love animals, or at least feel comfortable with them. Kelly likes to dress casually, so she would enjoy this job because working around animals requires casual clothes. Being shy is no problem either, because she will be working with pets more than with people.

3. Answer = d

   A summer camp counselor must like children, and should be used to outdoor activities like camping.

4. Answer = a or d

   Working at a book store or being a tutor will work best for Kim. People who love to read would most likely enjoy working in a book store. Kim also loves to teach, so she would probably enjoy tutoring another student.

Step 2: → Create Your Résumé

Résumés created by young people often contain information mainly about school activities. As you get older, your résumé will include more information about your work experience.

Employers like it when you bring a résumé when you apply for a job! Most jobs you apply for won't require a résumé, but submitting one increases your chances of getting the job. A résumé makes a good impression and shows your desire to make an extra effort in your job search. In order to impress employers with the effort that you put into your résumé, pay attention to the following guidelines. Your résumé should:

O   be typed on white typing paper;

O   be short and honest;

O   be neat and clean (no stains, smudges, wrinkles, rips); and

O   be free of spelling, grammar, and punctuation mistakes.

Let's talk about what goes on a résumé.

◆   Your name, address, phone number (including area code), and e-mail address if you have one.

◆   The name of the high school you attend, along with the year you will graduate.

◆   Languages, other than English, that you speak well.

◆   Work experience

o   This might include activities such as baby-sitting, odd jobs, or work in your school's office, library, or cafeteria.

◆   Volunteer work.

◆   School awards or honors.

◆ Job skills (for example, typing, computer, or other office skills).

◆ School activities such as sports, clubs, or cheerleading.

◆ Relevant interests and/or hobbies.

◆ At least three references—perhaps teachers, members of your church, friends of the family, or parents of friends.

    o   Your references must be adults.
    o   References should not be family members.
    o   You must have your references' permission before using their names.
    o   References should be typed on a separate sheet of paper, not on the same paper as your résumé.

Now you need to know what NOT to put on a résumé.

◆ Age

◆ Race

◆ Sex

◆ Physical descriptions such as height and weight or hair and eye color

◆ Religion

◆ Citizenship

One reason these details aren't included on a résumé is that they usually have nothing to do with your ability to perform the work. Another reason is that it is illegal for employers to discriminate against you based on any of the above characteristics unless they are relevant to the job. For example, to become a police officer you must be a certain age and height.

There are several different types and styles of résumés. The two types shown in this book (see examples on pages 9 and 10) are usually most effective for young people with little or no work experience.

If you want to see other résumé formats, you can go to a library and get more information. Just check the catalog subject guide under the heading résumé. You may also find some other examples on the Internet.

After you complete your résumé, have it checked by a teacher or school counselor before you give it to an employer. If you're applying for a job at more than one company, make sure you have made several copies of your résumé. Otherwise, you will have to type a new one for each employer.

TIP: Make sure that you have good clear copies of your résumé. You might ask a teacher where you can get the best copies made.

Along with your résumé, you might consider providing potential employers with a letter of recommendation (see example on page 11). This is a short letter that explains why you would be a good employee. A teacher or an adult other than your parent or guardian should write this letter.

The letter should contain facts about you—for example, that you are honest, loyal, a fast learner, or work well with other people. It should also tell employers how long each person has known you and how you met. You can attach this letter to your résumé.

*terms in bold are defined in the Glossary, page 103

SAMPLE RESUME 1

Linda Phillips
Anywhere, California 90008
(310) 555-1212
Email: lphillips@home.net

WORK EXPERIENCE

January 2018 to present: Clerk at Kelso High School office. My duties include filing, typing student permits, and some computer work.

June 2017 to present: Child Care: This position of trust involved general baby-sitting duties for children from ages 2 – 10 years. The care included meals or snacks as required. Also provided fun 'parent-approved' activities to entertain the children while they were in my care.

EDUCATION

Junior at Kelso High School. Graduating with the class of 2019.

HONORS

Dean's Honor List: 2015-2018.

INTERESTS

Computers: Completed two Microsoft Office programs (Word & Excel).

Music: Taking private piano lessons since 2005.

EXTRA-CURRICULAR ACTIVITIES

Captain of the girl's basketball team since 2017.
Assistant editor, Kelso High School Newsletter, 2018 to present.

REFERENCES PROVIDED ON REQUEST

SAMPLE RESUME 2

Kent Carlos

Anywhere, USA 08618
(609) 555-1212
Email: kcarlos@home.net

EDUCATION

Currently attending San Gabriel High School. Will be graduating in 2019. Enrolled in honors pre-calculus, chemistry, honors English, Spanish 8 (4th year), debate, and tennis. Held a 4.0 grade point average for three semesters in high school.

SKILLS

Type 40 words per minute. Very willing to learn other professional skills. Proficient in Microsoft Power Point.

LANGUAGES

Fluent in English, Spanish, Taiwanese and Mandarin. English is my native language. Learned to speak Spanish while living in Spain for 10 years. Learned Taiwanese and Mandarin while living in Taiwan for 4 years.

AWARDS

Faculty Honor List: 2016-2019

ACTIVITIES

Member of SGA (Student Government Association), Spanish Club, Varsity Tennis, and the Varsity Debate Team. Treasurer of Courtesy Committee and president of the Key Club.

INTERESTS

Interests include drawing, tennis, reading, travel, engineering, computers, and foreign languages.

REFERENCES PROVIDED ON REQUEST

EXAMPLE

LETTER OF RECOMMENDATION

January 25, 2019

Ilene John
4000 General Street
Los Angeles, CA 90000

To Whom It May Concern:

I have known Mary Doe for eight years. During this period she has demonstrated that she is a very honest and reliable person. She has been my baby-sitter for two years; she has not missed a day during this period and is always on time.

Mary has been very helpful with my children; and, because of her outgoing personality, they have requested that she be their only baby-sitter. During the time she has been working for me, she has maintained excellent grades in school.

I would highly recommend her for any job she applies for because of her good judgment and prior proven work habits.

Sincerely yours,

Ilene John

Step 2 → Review

1. You should have a one-page résumé.

    True ☐   False ☐

2. Employers don't mind a few fried-chicken grease stains on your résumé.

    True ☐   False ☐

3. Your résumé should be brief and honest.

    True ☐   False ☐

4. A résumé can make a good impression on employers.

    True ☐   False ☐

5. List three things that should be on a résumé.

    A. _____

    B. _____

    C. _____

6. List three things that you should not put on a résumé.

    A. _____

    B. _____

    C. _____

7. Give one good reason why you should have a résumé.

    _____

8. It's okay for your parent or guardian to write a letter of recommendation for you.

    True ☐   False ☐

COMPLETE THIS BLANK RÉSUMÉ

Name   _____

Address   _____

City/State/Zip _____

Phone   _____

E-mail Address _____

WORK EXPERIENCE

_____

_____

SKILLS

_____

_____

EDUCATION

_____

_____

HONORS

_____

_____

INTERESTS

_____

_____

EXTRACURRICULAR ACTIVITIES

_____

Step 2 → Answers

1. True

2. False

3. True

4. True

5. Any three of the following:

   1. Your name, address, phone number (including area code), and e-mail address
   2. Your high school's name and the year that you will graduate
   3. Languages, besides English, you speak well
   4. Skills
   5. Work experience
   6. Volunteer work
   7. School honors and awards
   8. After-school (extracurricular) activities
   9. Interests
   10. References

6. Any three of the following:

   1. Age
   2. Race
   3. Color of hair or eyes
   4. Sex (gender)
   5. Height and weight
   6. Religion
   7. Citizenship

7. Any one of the following:
   1. Employers like it when you bring a résumé
   2. Résumés make a good impression on employers

8. False

Step 3: → Look for Job Openings

Now let's talk about where to look for a job. Family and friends can sometimes tell you about places that are hiring. You might even pass by businesses that have a "NOW HIRING" sign out front. But there are other places to go when you are job hunting. Some of the most helpful are listed below.

The Internet: many jobs can be found there if you have access to a computer.

The classified ads section ("Want Ads") of the news paper is a good place to look (see sample on page19). You want to look in the employment section of the classified ads. Here is an important tip: the employment section is in alphabetical order. This means that a job that starts with a C (for example, Cashier) would be found before a job that started with an S (for example, Salesperson).

Employment agencies are another place to look for a job. Their staff can interview you and then set up an appointment with a company that is hiring. Young people should check with agencies that handle temporary and part-time jobs. Most agencies will not charge you for their help, but be sure to ask whether it will cost you any money. You can find employment agencies listed in the yellow pages of a telephone book under "Employment."

Your high school guidance or career center is another good place to find out about jobs. Sometimes jobs near your school will be listed on the bulletin boards. It's also a good idea to speak to a counselor at school for help with job hunting.

Another helpful place would be large companies. They may have free books or brochures about jobs with their company. This information will tell you about entry-level job openings. An entry-level job opening is a job for someone with little or no work experience. They will also let you know about jobs for people with various levels of work experience. You can call their employment offices or Human Resources (HR) departments for information.

Finally, there is the Employment Development Department (EDD) listed in the white pages of the telephone book under State Government. There are many jobs that you can choose from, and the staff can help you in your job search.

TIP: The places mentioned in this section are not the only places to find out about jobs, but they will give you a great start. Good luck!

Sample Classified Ad Section

Step 3 → Review

1. If you were looking for a job in the classified ads section ("Want Ads") of the newspaper, how would the jobs be listed?

    a.   By zip codes

    b.   By employers' names

    c.   Alphabetical order

    d.   By company address

2. List two places for job hunting.

    a.   _____

    b.   _____

3. If you want an employment agency to help you find a job, what question should you ask first?

    a.   Where are they located?

    b.   Are they good at finding jobs?

    c.   Are they friendly?

    d.   Will it cost you any money?

4. There is a good chance that your school can help you find a job. Which department should you check?

    a.   Cafeteria

    b.   Physical Education

    c.   High School Guidance or Career Center

    d.   Music Department

5. If you call a large company and need information about entry-level job openings, which department should you call?

    a.   Human Resources (HR)

    b.   Insurance

    c.   Accounting

    d.   Advertising

6. An entry-level job is for someone with only a little work experience.

    True ☐   False ☐

7. The places listed in Step 3 are the only ones where you can find out about jobs.

    True ☐   False ☐

Step 3 → Answers

1. c

2. Any two of the following:

    ◆ The classified section of the newspaper

    ◆ Employment agencies

    ◆ High school guidance or career center

    ◆ Large companies

    ◆ Employment Development Department (EDD)

    ◆ Internet

3. d

4. c

5. a

6. True

7. False

Step 4: → Dress for Job Hunting

How you dress can be very important when you are looking for a job. You should always try to make a good impression. To put it simply, you never get a second chance to make a first impression! A first impression is a terrible thing to waste!

Let's begin by suggesting what not to wear:

◆ Hats or caps

◆ Unconventional hair styles

◆ Heavy makeup

◆ Sunglasses

◆ Hair rollers

◆ Lots of jewelry (for example, four rings and big earrings)

◆ Sportswear, including tennis shoes, shorts, stretch pants, sweat suits, head bands, T-shirts, and tank tops

◆ Minidresses or miniskirts

◆ Dresses or skirts with thigh-high "slits"

◆ Jeans

◆ Sandals

◆ Tube or halter tops

◆ Formal wear, such as tuxedos or evening gowns

◆ Long and/or dirty fingernails. Fingernails should not be longer than one inch, and should be clean. If nails are polished, make sure the polish is not chipped.

◆ Very tight clothing

◆ Boots not covered by pants' cuffs

◆ Shoe or boot accessories such as buckles, straps, or spurs

◆ Lace or fishnet stockings

A good thing to keep in mind is that the way you might dress to go to a party, the park, or the mall is not the way to dress when job hunting. The next time you go to a mall or shopping center, look at how the employees are dressed. Unless they are working at a place that sells some of the things mentioned above, you will notice most employees dress a certain way.

Just as an experiment, start looking at how employees are dressed everywhere you go for one week. Begin at school: look at how the teachers, principals, and office workers dress. Some places, like the school cafeteria, will have employees in uniform. Watching how people are dressed will help you get ready for your job search.

Here is what you should wear:

Ladies:

- A nice dress, skirt, or pair of slacks in a subtle color

- Dress shoes with heels no higher than two inches

- Minimal makeup and jewelry (the less the better)

Men:

- A dress shirt in a subtle color

- A pair of slacks in black, brown, tan, gray, or navy blue

- A tie which matches your shirt and slacks

- Dress shoes in black, brown, tan, gray, or navy blue—depending on the color of your slacks

For All Job Seekers:

- Make sure that you and your clothes are clean.

- If you wear glasses, clean the lenses.

- Take the time to comb and style your hair neatly.

Dressing the right way is very important. You have a better chance of getting a job if the employer likes the way you look. This might surprise you, but many employers feel that casual or sloppy applicants may not have a good attitude toward their jobs if they are hired.

So, if you happen to be out shopping and see a "Now Hiring" sign, it's okay to stop and ask for an application to fill out at home. But be sure to mention that you just happen to be passing by. This way, if you are wearing shorts and a T-shirt, you won't give the impression that your appearance is not important to you.

When you take the application back to the employer, make sure that you are dressed properly. If, after turning in your application, the employer asks you to come back for an interview, make sure that your are well groomed, as discussed above.

TIP: Your clothes may not represent "the real you," but don't let an unprofessional appearance ruin your chances of being seen as a good person to hire.

Step 4 → Review

1. Which three of the following should not be worn when job hunting?

    a. Sandals
    b. White shirt
    c. Jeans
    d. Dress flats
    e. Slacks
    f. Shorts

2. Which was mentioned as a good place to go see how people dress when they are at work?

    a. The park
    b. A party
    c. The mall
    d. Church
    e. A theater

3. List three items that young women should wear when job hunting.

    a. _____

    b. _____

    c. _____

4. List three items that young men should wear when job hunting.

    a. _____

    b. _____

    c. _____

5. How you are dressed when job hunting can be very important.

    True ☐   False ☐

6. It is best if you and your clothes are clean.

    True ☐   False ☐

Step 4 → Answers

1. a, c, f

2. c

3. Any three of the following:

    ◆   A nice dress
    ◆   Dress flats or shoes with 2-inch or lower heels
    ◆   A skirt
    ◆   Slacks
    ◆   A nice blouse
    ◆   Minimal makeup and jewelry

4. Any three of the following:

    ◆   A shirt
    ◆   A tie
    ◆   Slacks
    ◆   Dress shoes

5. True

6. True

Step 5: → Know Your Terms I:
The Application for Employment

See the sample application on pages 49 and 50 after studying the following words.

1. ACCOMMODATE: To make suitable, to provide with something needed.

   The application might ask, "What can be done to ACCOMMODATE a problem or limitation that you have?" For example, if you are in a wheelchair, what can be done to help you in the workplace?

2. APPLICANT'S NAME: The name of the person looking for a job.

   Note: Simply print your name in the space.

3. ALIEN: From another country.

   The application might ask, "Are you a U.S. citizen, or an ALIEN?" Which means, "Are you a citizen of the United States of America, or are you from another country?"

4. AUTHORIZED: Having permission to do something.

   The application might ask, "Are you either a U.S. citizen or an alien AUTHORIZED to work in the United States?" Which means, "If you are not a United States citizen, do you have legal permission to work in this country?"

5. CERTIFY: To say or agree in writing that something is true.

   The section just before the space for your signature may say, "I CERTIFY that the facts in this application are true and complete." This means that by signing the application you are saying that everything you wrote is true.

6. CONTRARY: Something that is different or opposite.

    The application may say, "No representative of the company has authority to make a CONTRARY agreement." This means that no representative of the company can make a promise different from what the application says.

7. CONVICTION RECORD: The official record with the police or courts stating that an applicant has been found guilty of a crime.

    The application might say, "You will not be denied employment solely because of a CONVICTION RECORD, unless the offense is related to the job for which you have applied." Which means, "If the crime you have been convicted of has nothing to do with the job you are applying for, you might get the job."

8. DISABILITY: A physical weakness, illness, or condition. For instance, a broken arm is a disability, and a person who is blind has a disability.

    The application may say, "This waiver does not permit the release or use of DISABILITY-related or medical information…" This means the application does not allow the company to give out information concerning your physical condition.

9. DISCRIMINATION: When someone or something is not treated the same as someone else or something else.

    The application may say, "We are an equal opportunity employer; we will not DISCRIMINATE based on race, sex, religion, or citizenship." This means they cannot refuse to hire applicants for these reasons.

10. DISMISSAL: Being fired or let go from a job.

    The employment application says, "Falsified statements on this application shall be grounds for dismissal." This means that if you wrote something false on the application, you can be fired.

11. FALSIFIED: Refers to something that is not true or to tell a lie.

    The employment application says "falsified statements on this application shall be grounds for dismissal." This means that if you lied on the application, you can be fired.

12. FELONY: A serious crime which usually results in a prison sentence.

The application may ask, "Have you been convicted of a FELONY?" This means, "Have you been found guilty of a serious crime?"

13. FLUENTLY: To speak a language easily or very well.

The application might say, "What foreign languages do you speak FLUENTLY?" This means, "What languages other than English do you speak very well?"

14. FOREGOING: Previous or earlier.

The application may say that applicants cannot "make any agreement contrary to the FOREGOING," which means to make any promises different from what they've already said on the application.

15. INQUIRE: To ask questions.

The application might ask, "Are you employed now, and if so may we INQUIRE of your present employer?" This means, "If you are working now, may we ask your employer questions about you?"

16. INVESTIGATION: The process of searching, exploring, or looking into.

The application may say, "I authorize INVESTIGATION of all statements contained herein," which means, "You permit the company to check out everything you wrote on the application."

17. JOB TITLE: Refers to the name of any job that you have held. Some applications may show POSITION TITLE instead of JOB TITLE.

For example, if you worked in a department store, your JOB TITLE may have been Cashier.

18. LIABILITY: Legal responsibility.

After asking for your permission to investigate your employment history, the application may ask you to "release the company from all LIABILITY for any damage that may result from utilization of such information." This means that you free the company from all legal responsibility for any problems that may come up for you when they check out what you wrote on your application.

19. LIMITATION: Something that will stop you from being able to do certain things.

The application might ask, "Do you have any physical LIMITATIONS?" For example, being blind or deaf (unable to hear) can stop you from being able to do certain jobs.

20. MISDEMEANOR: A crime that is less serious than a FELONY (see word #12). This kind of crime is often punished with a fine and/or time served in a county jail rather than a prison.

The application might ask, "Have you ever been convicted of a MISDEMEANOR?" This is asking if you have been found guilty of crime that is not as serious as a felony.

21. NOTIFY: To give notice to, to call or write to.

The application might say, "In case of emergency NOTIFY_____." The application is asking who the company should tell if there is an emergency at work. For instance, if you get sick at work, who should the employer call? Most young people will write the names of a parent or guardian.

22. PERMANENT ADDRESS: A place where you receive mail, or a place that you own or rent. Sometimes this applies to a P.O. BOX (post office box).

The application will ask that you write your PERMANENT ADDRESS in the space provided. This means, "Write the address where you live and/or receive mail."

23. PERTINENT: Pertaining to, related to the matter being considered, important.

The application might ask for your permission to obtain information, "concerning my previous employment and any PERTINENT information, personal or otherwise." This refers to information concerning your past jobs and any important personal or other information they may have about you. For example, the new employer may want to find out if you got along with everyone or find out if you had good attendance at your past job.

24. PRECLUDE: To prevent, to make impossible, to stop.

The application might ask, "Do you have any physical LIMITATIONS (see word #19) that would PRECLUDE you from performing any work for which you are being considered?" Which means, "Do you have any physical conditions that will make it impossible for you to do this work?"

25. PRESENT ADDRESS: The place where you live now.

   The application will simply ask for your PRESENT ADDRESS, which means, "Write the address of the place you are living."

26. PRIOR: Earlier, in advance.

   The application might ask you to agree with the statement that, "I may be TERMINATED (see word #31), at any time without PRIOR notice." This means that you can lose your job without any warning.

27. PROHIBIT: To stop someone from doing something.

   The application might say that, "The Employment Act of 1967 PROHIBITS DISCRIMATION (see word #9) on the basis of age," which means that an employer can't use age as a reason for not hiring someone.

28. RANK: Refers to the name, class, or level held while in the Military Services.

   The application is asking you to write the name of the position you held if you were in the military. For instance, you may have been a Private-First Class. If you were never in the military, just write N/A in that space. N/A stands for "Not Applicable" and means that a question does not apply to you.

29. REFERENCES: This refers to people who can tell someone about you—for instance, "What kind of person you are and what kind of work habits you have."

   The application may have a space where you're asked about REFERENCES. You will need to list the name, address, and telephone numbers of 3-4 people who have known you at least one year and are not relatives.

30. REFERRED BY: Refers to the person who told you about the job for which you're applying.

   The application may have a space where you're asked who REFERRED you for the job. If it's applicable, give the name of the person who told you about the job.

31. TERMINATED: To be fired.

   The application might ask you to agree that, under certain conditions, "I may be TERMINATED." This means that you can be fired.

32. TRADE SCHOOL: Refers to a school (not high school) that teaches or trains its students in certain skills or trades. Some applications may call it CORRESPONDENCE or VOCATIONAL SCHOOL.

The application may have a space under Education that asks you to list TRADE, CORRESPONDENCE, or OTHER BUSINESS schools that you have attended.

33. UTILIZATION: Use of, using.

The application may say, "…and release the company from all liability for any damage that may result from UTILIZATION of such information." Which means the company is free from legal blame for any problems that come up for you when they check out what you wrote on your application.

34. WAIVER: A type of permission.

After asking for your permission to find certain information, the application might claim, for example, that "this WAIVER does not permit the release or use of disability-related or medical information." This means that although you have given your employer permission to find information, your employer cannot use or share this information with anyone else.

35. WORK HISTORY: Refers to work you have done in the past. Some applications may show this as EMPLOYMENT HISTORY.

The application is asking you to list information about jobs that you may have held in the past They will want to know things like job title, dates worked, name of employer, address, and duties performed.

> TIP: Words are your friends. Try to learn a new word each day—these friends can change your life.

Step 5 → Review

Match the words to the correct meaning below.

1. ___ACCOMMODATE

2. ___AUTHORIZED

3. ___APPLICANT'S NAME

4. ___CERTIFY

5. ___CONTRARY

6. ___DISABILITY

7. ___DISCRIMINATION

8. ___DISMISSAL

9. ___FALSIFIED

10. ___FLUENTLY

11. ___JOB TITLE

12. ___LIABILITY

13. ___LIMITATION

14. ___RANK

15. ___INVESTIGATION

16. ___UTILIZATION

17. ___PERTINENT

18. ___REFERRED BY

19. ___TRADE SCHOOL

20. ___WORK HISTORY

A. Something that is opposite or different.
B. Refers to the name, class, or level held in the Military Services.
C. To have permission to do something.
D. Legal responsibility.
E. To speak a language easily or very well.
F. To be fired or let go from a job.
G. Refers to something that is not true or to telling a lie.
H. To search, explore, look into, or investigate.
I. To use.
J. Pertaining to, related to the matter being considered, important.
K. Something that will stop you from being able to do certain things.
L. The person who told you about the job for which you're applying.
M. To say or agree in writing that something is true.
N. Refers to the name of the person looking for a job.

O. To make suitable, to provide with something needed.
P. A physical weakness, illness, or condition.
Q. Someone or something is treated differently from someone or something else.
R. Refers to the name of any job that you have held.
S. Refers to work you have done in the past.
T. Refers to a school that teaches certain skills or trades.

Step 5 → Answers

1. O
2. C
3. N
4. M
5. A
6. P
7. Q
8. F
9. G
10. E
11. R
12. D
13. K
14. B
15. H
16. I
17. J
18. L
19. T
20. S

Step 6: → Complete the Application for Employment

Most employers will have you fill out an EMPLOYMENT APPLICATION before they hire you for a job. An employment application is a form that tells the employer about you and your work history. Many of the questions it will ask are very easy to answer. For instance:

◆ What is your name?

◆ Where do you live?

◆ What schools have you attended?

◆ Have you worked before?

These are only a few of the questions that will be asked. You will fill out a sample application later on, and it will give you a better idea of the other questions that you may need to answer.

Make sure that you are ready to fill out the application by having the following:

1. A pen with black or blue ink. Do not use a pencil.

2. A social security card. (You can get a card from the Social Security Administration.) See page 46.

3. A green card (for noncitizens only.)

4. A list of high schools that you have gone to and their addresses.

5. A list of any jobs you have had: you need the employer's name, address, supervisor's name, and company phone number.

   ◆ Note. You should mention school jobs like working in the school's office or cafeteria—these are important too.

6. A small pocket dictionary. Spelling is important on an application! Poor spelling looks bad; an employer may not hire you because of it.

7. A list of two or three personal references, such as teachers or family friends, along with their addresses and phone numbers. These must be people other than relatives, whom you have known for at least one year. <u>Do not list anyone as a reference unless they say it is okay!</u>

Getting a Social Security Card

Your social security number is a nine-digit account number. Each person is given a different number. No two numbers are the same. The number looks like this: 546-00-1234

The social security card is a card issued by the federal government; in fact it is the Social Security Administration who will issue the card. Ask your parent or guardian if you have a social security number. Sometimes children are issued a card as early as the age of one if a parent or guardian applies for it.

If you don't have a card, you can call the Social Security Administration and ask them what you need to do in order to get a social security number. You can search for them on the Internet or by checking the White Pages of your local telephone book.

Filling Out the Employment Application—Sample on pages 49 and 50

- ◆ Read all instructions before completing the application.
- ◆ Use an ink pen (black or blue ink only)
- ◆ Print very neatly
- ◆ Complete all sections of the application

One of the most important things about filling out an application is following instructions! If the application says print, then you must print.

The application is the first thing that employers use to see if you can follow simple directions. They also use it to learn more about you before they talk to you in an interview.

Be sure to fill out your application neatly. Some employers get hundreds of applications each month. They may not waste time trying to figure out what you wrote!

Once you start filling out the application, you will likely notice that, because of your age and experience, not all the questions will be relevant to you. When there is information on the application you do not need to fill out, write N/A. This means NOT APPLICABLE. Never leave a question blank, because the employer needs to know why you skipped it. Putting N/A clearly tells them that the question did not apply to you.

Keep in mind that, no matter how old you are, some of the questions will <u>never</u> apply to you; however, the rule remains the same: put N/A on those lines.

After you have finished the application, look at it carefully and make sure all sections are filled out before you turn it in. Some applications are two-sided (they have questions on the front and back), so be sure to check both sides!

Here is a helpful tip: If an employer lets you take the application home to fill out, make sure you keep it clean. Don't get food stains, grease, or other marks on it!

A final, and important, tip for filling out an application: never write the amount of money you expect to make in the salary section. You should answer this section with "open," because it will allow the employer to tell you what amount they are planning to pay you. The employer may have already decided to pay you a higher amount than you would have asked for.

TIP: If people have told you that your writing is hard to read, practice writing until it is clear. You can do it!

Sample Application Form—Page 1

Standard Application for Employment

It is our policy to comply with all applicable state and federal laws prohibiting discrimination in employment based on race, age, color, sex, religion, national origin, disability or other protected classifications.

Please carefully read and answer all questions. You will not be considered for employment if you fail to completely answer all the questions on this application. You may attach a résumé, but all questions must be answered.

"Employer"	Position applying for

PERSONAL DATA

Name (last, first, middle)

Street Address and/or Mailing Address	City	State	Zip

Home Telephone Number	Business Telephone Number	Cellular Telephone Number

Date you can start work	Salary Desired	Do you have a High School Diploma or GED? Yes ☐ No ☐

POSITION INFORMATION   Check all that you are willing to work

Hours: Full Time ☐ Part Time ☐	Days ☐ Evenings ☐	Swing ☐ Graveyard ☐ Weekends ☐	Status: Regular ☐ Temporary ☐

Are you authorized to work in the U.S. on an unrestricted basis?	Yes ☐	No ☐

Have you ever been convicted of a felony? (Convictions will not necessarily disqualify an applicant for employment.)   Yes ☐   No ☐

If yes, explain:

Have you been told the essential functions of the job or have you been viewed a copy of the job description listing the essential functions of the job?
Yes ☐   No ☐

Can you perform these essential functions of the job with or without reasonable accommodation?   Yes ☐   No ☐

QUALIFICATIONS   Please list any education or training you feel relates to the position applied for that would help you perform the work, such as schools, colleges, degrees, vocational or technical programs, and military training.

	School Name	Degree	Address/City/State
School			
School			
Other			

SPECIAL SKILLS   List any special skills or experience that you feel would help you in the position that you are applying for (leadership, organizations/teams, etc.

REFERENCES   Please list three professional references not related to you, with full name, address, phone number, and relationship. If you don't have three professional references, then list personal, unrelated references.

Name	Address/City/State	Phone	Relationship

Sample Application Form—Page 2

WORK HISTORY Start with your present or most recent employment and work back. Use separate sheet if necessary. (INCLUDE PAID AND UNPAID POSITIONS)		
Job Title #1	Start Date (mo/day/yr)	End Date (mo/day/yr)
Company Name	Supervisor's Name	Phone Number
City	State	Zip
Duties:		
Reason for Leaving	Starting Salary	Ending Salary

May we contact your present employer?   Yes ☐   No ☐   N/A ☐

Job Title #2	Start Date (mo/day/yr)	End Date (mo/day/yr)
Company Name	Supervisor's Name	Phone Number
City	State	Zip
Duties:		
Reason for Leaving	Starting Salary	Ending Salary

Job Title #3	Start Date (mo/day/yr)	End Date (mo/day/yr)
Company Name	Supervisor's Name	Phone Number
City	State	Zip
Duties:		
Reason for Leaving	Starting Salary	Ending Salary

Job Title #4	Start Date (mo/day/yr)	End Date (mo/day/yr)
Company Name	Supervisor's Name	Phone Number
City	State	Zip
Duties:		
Reason for Leaving	Starting Salary	Ending Salary

I certify that the facts set forth in this Application for Employment are true and complete to the best of my knowledge. I understand that if I am employed, false statements, omissions or misrepresentations may result in my dismissal. I authorize the Employer to make an investigation of any of the facts set forth in this application and release the Employer from any liability. The employer may contact any listed references on this application.

I acknowledge and understand that the company is an "at will" employer. Therefore, any employee (regular, temporary, or other type of category employee) may resign at any time, just as the employer may terminate the employment relationship with any employee at any time, with or without cause, with or without notice to the other party.

_____   _____
Applicant Signature   Date

Step 6 → Review

Complete the following "True" or "False" quiz. Check the correct answers.

1. Most employers will give you an employment application to fill out.

    True ☐   False ☐

2. As a U.S. citizen you must have a social security number and a green card.

    True ☐   False ☐

3. You can use a pen or a pencil to fill out the employment application.

    True ☐   Falsc ☐

4. Concerning personal references, it is okay to list someone as a reference without telling them.

    True ☐   False ☐

5. Applications should be filled out with a red ink pen.

    True ☐   False ☐

6. The employer can provide you with a social security card.

    True ☐   False ☐

7. No two social security numbers are the same.

    True ☐   False ☐

8. The federal government issues one social security number.

    True ☐   False ☐

9. There are 10 numbers in a social security number.

    True ☐   False ☐

10. When filling out an application, it is important to follow instructions.

    True ☐   False ☐

11. When you write N/A on your application it means "not applicable."

    True ☐   False ☐

12. It is okay to leave blank spaces on an application.

    True ☐   False ☐

13. If you take the application home to fill out, it is good to keep it clean and free of stains and grease.

    True ☐   False ☐

14. It is a good idea to write "open" in the salary section of the application.

    True ☐   False ☐

Step 6 → Answers

1. True

2. False

3. False

4. False

5. False

6. False

7. True

8. True

9. False

10. True

11. True

12. False

13. True

14. True

Step 7: → Know Your Terms II: The Interview

While searching or being interviewed for a job, you can be sure that you will come face to face with new words. You may also find these words on employment applications, questionnaires, or tests.

You might be asked questions during an interview which you won't be able to answer—because you are not sure what you were asked!

Don't worry, because the words below are words that are likely to be used in interviews.

1. ABILITY: Being able to do something.

    You might be asked, "Do you have the ABILITY to do this type of work?" This means, "Are you able to do the work?"

2. ACCOMPLISHMENT: Something that you have done.

    You might be asked, "Do you have any ACCOMPLISHMENTS that relate to this job?" This means, "Have you done anything or been involved in anything that is like this kind of work?"

3. ASSET: Something of value.

    You might be asked, "What ASSETS do you have that might make you a good choice for this job?" This means, "What is good about you that would make this company want to hire you?"

    Good grades, a good attendance record, a helpful attitude, and the desire to do a good job are examples of ASSETS employers might consider valuable.

4. ATTIRE: How you are dressed.

You might be told, "Your ATTIRE will be very important if you get this job." This means, "How you are dressed will be important if you get the job."

5. AUTHORITY: A person or group of persons in control (the boss).

    You might be asked, "Do you have any trouble adjusting to AUTHORITY?" This means, "Is it a problem for you when someone in charge tells you what to do?"

6. CANDIDATE: A person who seeks a certain job or office.

    You might be asked, "What makes you a good CANDIDATE for this job?" This means, "Why would this company want to hire you for this job?"

7. CONTRIBUTION: Something that is given or done to help a common cause or result.

    You might be asked, "What CONTRIBUTIONS did you make to the club you were a member of?" Which means, "What have you done as a member of your club to help it achieve its goals?" For example, if your club was having a dance and you sold tickets, the help you gave was "sales." Or perhaps you were the "treasurer" in charge of keeping a record of all the money.

8. CURRICULUM: Subjects or courses of study at a school.

    You might be asked, "Do you feel that your CURRICULUM has prepared you for this job?" This means, "Have the classes you are taking in school prepared you for this job?"

9. DISCIPLINARY ACTION: A method used to enforce a company rule or policy.

    You might be told, "If you do not follow company rules, DISCIPLINARY ACTION may be taken." This means, "If you break company rules, something you don't like will be done to you." For example, you could receive a warning or be fired.

10. DUTIES PERFORMED: The main work done at your job.

    You might be told, "Tell me about the DUTIES PERFORMED at your last job," which means, "Tell me about the type of work you did at your last job."

11. EVALUATION: A report that tells you how well you are performing on the job.

    You might be told, "You will have an EVALUATION every three months," which means, "Every three months your employer will let you know if you are doing a good or poor job."

12. EXTRACURRICULAR: Activities or studies that are not included in the subjects or courses that you are taking in school.

You might be asked, "In what EXTRACURRICULAR activities have you been active?" This means, "What activities have you been a part of that have nothing to do with your school classes?" For example, if you were active in sports, school clubs, community work, or outside clubs like the YMCA or YWCA, then be sure to tell the interviewer about these activities.

13. GOAL: Something you are trying to achieve or do.

You might be asked, "What are your GOALS for the near future?" which could mean, "What do you want to complete or reach in the next few months or years?" For example, your goal might be to get a job as a cashier and try to become a manager's assistant within a few months. Or your goal may be to work part-time to help pay your way through college.

14. OCCUPATION: Job or work.

You might be asked, "What OCCUPATION are you interested in?" Which means, "What type of work do you want to do?"

15. QUALIFICATION: A talent or skill; the training or preparation necessary to do something.

You might be asked, "What QUALIFICATIONS do you have for this job?" Which means, "Tell me what training or skills you have that you can use for this job?"

16. RECOMMENDATION: To speak or write well of; to say good things about a person.

You might be asked, "If I call one of your teachers, will he or she give you a good RECOMMENDATION?" This means, "If I call your teacher will the teacher say good things about you?"

17. REFERENCES: People who are not your relatives, and who will tell the truth about you. For instance, they might say that you are honest, dependable, friendly, or have a good attitude.

You might be told, "Please provide three personal REFERENCES," which means that you need to provide the name, address, and phone number of three people (not relatives) who can tell the employer what kind of person you are.

Special Tip: Never use someone as a reference before getting his or her okay! Be sure to tell them you need a reference because you are looking for a job. Let them know someone might call.

18. RESPONSIBILITY: Being responsible; a duty.

You might be asked, "What was your RESPONSIBILITY as a baby-sitter?" Your answers might include things like: feeding the children, reading to them, and putting them to bed.

19. RÉSUMÉ: A written statement of facts about a person's school and work background.

You might be asked, "Do you have a résumé?" See Step 2, Create Your Résumé, for more details.

20. SALARY: The money you are paid for working; wages.

You might be asked, "What hourly SALARY are you looking to earn?" This means, "How much money do you want to make per hour?"

21. TERMINATE: To end your employment, to be fired from a job.

You might be asked, "Have you ever been TERMINATED from a job?" This means, "Have you ever been fired from a job?"

22. VOCATIONAL: Career or job related.

An interviewer might ask, "What is your VOCATIONAL goal?" This means, "What type of job are you looking for?"

Step 7: → Review

Match the words below to the correct meanings below.

1. ___RÉSUMÉ

2. ___REFERENCES

3. ___EVALUATION

4. ___QUALIFICATION

5. ___RECOMMENDATION

6. ___ATTIRE

7. ___CANDIDATE

8. ___CURRICULUM

9. ___ACCOMPLISHMENT

10. ___ABILITY

A. Something worthwhile that you have done.
B. Being able to do something.
C. How you are dressed.
D. A person who seeks a certain job or office.
E. Subjects or courses of study at a school.
F. A report that tells you how well you have performed on the job.
G. Being trained or prepared for something, having a talent or skill.
H. To speak or write well of; to say good things about a person.
I. People who are not your relatives who will tell the truth about you.
J. A written statement of a person's skills and accomplishments.

Step 7 → Answers

1. J

2. I

3. F

4. G

5. H

6. C

7. D

8. E

9. A

10. B

Step 8: → Present Yourself Effectively at the Interview

An INTERVIEW is a meeting between you and an employer. The purpose of the interview is for the employer to talk with you and learn more about you. You will find that most employers want to talk to you before they decide whether or not to hire you.

The interview will normally last less than 30 minutes, and the interviewer will ask most of the questions. This is where you get the chance to tell about yourself.

Good interviewers expect you to do most of the talking. Remember, they're trying to learn more about you. Therefore you should avoid quick "YES" or "NO" answers. For instance, if you are asked whether or not you like school, don't just say, "yes" and end it there. Tell the interviewer why you like school.

Let's talk a little more about answering questions. Here are some important hints for you to follow:

- ◆ Speak in a clear, easy-to-understand voice.

- ◆ Don't mumble!

- ◆ Avoid using "slang." (The interviewer may not know what you are talking about!)

- ◆ Be truthful. If you're not sure of an answer, admit it.

- ◆ Speak as if you know what you are talking about, and try to have a good attitude.

Now that you are ready to begin your interview, let's talk about GOOD EYE CONTACT. "What is that?" you might ask. Good eye contact is when you look into the eyes of the person talking to you. Good eye contact makes you look calm, and makes the interviewer feel that you are paying attention and are honest.

Don't get the wrong idea about good eye contact—you should not stare. It's okay to look around the room from time to time, but don't make a habit of it.

Think about times when you've talked to someone who was not paying attention to you. Do you remember being a little upset? Interviewers are no different. They want to know you are listening, and good eye contact helps them feel this way.

Here are some questions an interviewer might ask you:

1. Why do you want to work for this company?

2. Why are you looking for this kind of work?

3. Why do you feel you can do this type of work?

4. What do you see yourself doing when you complete high school?

5. What kind of grades do you have in school? (Be ready to explain your grades if they are not good.)

6. What are your strengths and weaknesses?

7. What hours can you work?

8. Do you have any questions?

Other Important Points:

◆   You should not be late for your interview.

◆   Plan to arrive about 15 minutes early.

o   Note: Most interviewers don't like for you to come too early, because they may be busy or have another person to interview!

Being late to an interview is one of the worst mistakes you can make when you are trying to get a job! Most interviewers feel that if you come late for your interview, you will come to work late after you're hired.

When you go to your interview, check in with whoever is in charge, unless you were told to report to a certain person or place. Be sure to tell the person who you are and why you are there. For example, you should say, "My name is Leslie Smith, and I have a 2:00 interview with Mr. Reed."

When the interviewer is ready to talk to you, you will be asked to come into their office and be seated. Follow these suggestions:

◆ Try not to be nervous!

◆ Shake interviewer's hand firmly to show confidence.

◆ Let the interviewer show you where to sit.

◆ Smile and look friendly!

◆ Sit up straight—no leaning or slouching.

◆ Rest your hands in your lap and relax. (Do not fold your arms together.)

Earlier it was mentioned that the interviewer might ask if you have any questions of your own. Most employers like it when the answer is "yes." Here are some good questions to ask:

◆ Do you feel that I can do this job?

◆ Do your employees wear a uniform?

◆ What kind of training is involved for the job?

◆ What hours will I be working if I am hired?

Now, let's talk about a few final points: Some employers will interview you the same day that you turn in your employment application. Others will choose to call you and set up an interview appointment after they have read your application. Here are some important tips to remember when you are waiting to hear from an employer:

◆ Tell anyone who normally answers the phone at home that you are looking for a job and waiting to hear from employers.

◆ Tell them to be sure they get the caller's name and phone number.

◆ Keep a pen and paper near the phone. Remember that you are expecting employers to call and should be ready. Don't keep them waiting while someone goes to find pen and paper.

◆ If <u>you</u> answer the phone, make sure to get the following information:

o   The date and time of the interview.

o   The exact location of the interview. (Be sure to get the directions and ask where you can park.)

o   Ask whom you should report to when you get there.

o   Ask for the name of the person who called to set up the interview.

o   Finally, ask for the phone number so that you can call later if you have questions.

TIP: If you find it hard to give good eye contact—try this instead: Look at the other person's nose!

Step 8 → Review

1. Give two tips to remember when you are waiting to hear from an employer:

    a. _____

    b. _____

2. What time should you be there for your interview?

    a. 30 minutes early

    b. 1 hour early

    c. 15 minutes early

    d. 5 minutes early

3. When the interviewer takes you into his or her office for the interview, list four things you should do:

    a. _____

    b. _____

    c. _____

    d. _____

4. It is okay to use slang during the interview.

    True ☐   False ☐

5. List three questions that you might ask the interviewer:

    a. _____

    b. _____

    c. _____

6. While job hunting, you should keep a pen and paper next to the phone.

    True ☐   False ☐

Step 8 → Answers

1. An y two of the following:

   ◆ Tell anyone who normally answers the phone at home that you are looking for a job and waiting to hear from employers.

   ◆ Make sure you tell them to get the caller's name and phone number.

   ◆ Keep a pen and paper near the phone.

   ◆ If <u>you</u> answer the phone, get complete information (date, time, exact location, whom to report to, caller's name, and phone number).

2. c

3. Any four of the following:

   ◆ Try not to be nervous!

   ◆ Shake interviewer's hand firmly (shows confidence).

   ◆ Let the interviewer show you where to sit.

   ◆ Smile and look friendly!

   ◆ Sit up straight (no leaning or slouching).

   ◆ Rest you hands in your lap and relax. (Do not fold your arms together.)

4. False

5. Any three of the following:

   ◆ Do you feel that I can do this job?

   ◆ Do I have to wear a uniform?

◆   Will I need any training?

◆   What hours will I be working if I am hired?

6. True

Step 9: → Know Your Interview Dos & Don'ts

This step will cover WHAT TO DO AND SAY, and WHAT NOT TO DO AND SAY, at an interview. Paying attention to this step can save you from some embarrassing moments and keep you from making some mistakes that might stop you from being hired.

When asked, "Why do you want to work for this company?"

◆ DO say, "I think it would be a good opportunity for me," or "I believe that I will enjoy this kind of work," or "I would like to learn something new."

◆ DON'T say, "I chose your company because I need a job," or "It's close to home," or "I need some money," or "My parents said I have to get a job!"

These last answers show that you just need a job and don't care where you work! The first answers show that you are interested in working for the specific company, which is very important to the person who is thinking about hiring you.

When looking for a job, you should find out exactly what type of work you will be doing. If the job will be working in a shoe store, find out if you will be a cashier or if you will put shoes on shelves and/or sell them.

◆ DO find out what you will be doing if you are hired. Employers like people who ask good questions. An interviewer will need to know when you can work, so before you go to the interview:

◆ DO write down the days and hours you can work. Remember your school schedule and any after-school activities you are involved in such as sports, study groups, clubs, or baby-sitting.

◆ DON'T say, "I can work any day after school," or "I can work as late as you need me to," unless you know this is true! Know when you can work! You may have to baby-sit two days a week, or your parents may want you to be home by 9:00 PM. That is why you need to write down this information before you talk to the employer. It gives you a chance to think about what hours you can work and to check with your parents about how late you can work. Also, if you get nervous and forget when you can work, all you have to do is look at what you have written down.

Remember that the question of how much money you will be making can be a "touchy subject." It's okay to ask about money, but there is a right way and a wrong way to do so. Employers want to believe that money isn't the only thing you are interested in. Therefore, make sure that you bring up the subject of your wages in a way that lets them know money is not the only reason that you want the job.

You might be thinking, "What's so bad about money being the reason?" Well, most employers want both the money and the job to be important to you. In fact, sometimes you won't get hired if money is the only reason you want the job.

◆ DO say, "May I ask about the salary?"

◆ DON'T say, "How much do you pay?" or "How much am I going to make?"

Now is a good time to mention an important fact: being interviewed does not mean that you will be hired!

After an interview is over, some interviewers will say, "We will call you and let you know our decision." Other companies will tell you during the interview if you will be hired. Sometimes they will let you know by mail if you are hired or not.

If the interviewer says, "We will let you know if you were hired,"

◆ DO ask, "When can I expect to hear from you?"

◆ DON'T ask, "Did I get the job?"

◆ DO call if they promise to reach you within a certain time but you do not hear from them. When you call, ask to speak to the person who interviewed you. Give him or her your name and the date you were interviewed, and ask if the company has come to a decision. If your interviewer says, "I am sorry, but you didn't get the job," politely say, "May I ask why?" The answer may help you in your next interview.

◆ DO thank them if they say, "Congratulations, you're hired!" Then ask, "When do I start?"

◆ DON'T have a parent, or anyone else, call and ask whether or not you're going to get the job! Employers expect you to be adult enough to make your own phone calls.

Here are a couple of other good tips to follow:

◆ DO come to the interview alone.

◆ DON'T bring family or friends to the interview! If others come with you, have them wait in the car or outside. Employers like to see that you can do things alone.

These are the final three points:

◆ DO answer all questions in a clear and relaxed voice.

◆ DON'T chew gum at the interview!

◆ DO bring a small note pad and pen. It will show that you are prepared to take down important points and are behaving in a businesslike way.

Step 9 → Review

1. Pick the best answer to give an interviewer who asks why you want the job.

    a. I need a job close to home.
    b. My parents said I have to get a job.
    c. I believe I will enjoy this type of work.

2. Employers like people who ask good questions during the interview.

    ☐ True ☐ False

3. There is a right way and a wrong way to ask employers how much money you will make.

    ☐ True ☐ False

4. It is okay to ask, "When can I expect to hear from you?"

    ☐ True ☐ False

5. If you want to know if you got the job, you should have a parent call the employer.

    ☐ True ☐ False

6. It's all right to bring your friends to the interview.

    ☐ True ☐ False

7. If you get hired, it's okay to ask, "When do I start?"

    ☐ True ☐ False

8. Being interviewed does not mean that you will be hired.

    ☐ True ☐ False

9. It's better to ask, "May I ask about the salary?" than "How much do you pay?"

    ☐ True   ☐ False

10. Employers expect you to be _____ enough to make your own phone calls.

Step 9 → Answers

1. c

2. True

3. True

4. True

5. False

6. False

7. True

8. True

9. True

10. Adult

Step 10: → Important Forms (Work Permit, Form I-9, & Form W-4)

Work Permit

Let's talk about the WORK PERMIT. The work permit is a Government form required by most States. An employer who hires a minor (someone under age 18) is legally required to have a work permit on file for that person.

In most cases, you must be at least 14 years of age to get a work permit. Although 14 and 15 year olds may get work permits, most employers will not hire students under 16.

The work permit was created to keep young people from working jobs that might not be safe, such as work related to fire fighting, manufacturing, or mining.

To get a work permit, you must attend school. The reason for this requirement is to make sure that minors stay in school and to prove that their parents or guardians have given permission for them to have jobs.

The work permit is also used to let employers know how many hours you're allowed to work each day and each week.

Steps to follow:

- Go to your high school's office or career education office and ask for a form called the "Statement of Intent to Employ a Minor and Request for Work Permit." This form must be completed in order for you to get a work permit (see sample forms on pages 83 and 84).

    - Note: If your school is closed for the summer or holidays, you can get the form from the school's district office.

- You should fill out the top part of the form. The new employer will complete the middle section. Your parent or legal guardian must sign the next section.

Page 1 of Statement of Intent to Employ

STATE OF CALIFORNIA DEPARTMENT OF EDUCATION
STATEMENT OF INTENT TO EMPLOY A MINOR AND REQUEST FOR A WORK PERMIT--CERTIFICATE OF AGE
CDE Form B1-1 (Rev. 02-14)

A "STATEMENT OF INTENT TO EMPLOY A MINOR AND REQUEST FOR A WORK PERMIT--CERTIFICATE OF AGE"
form (CDE Form B1-1) shall be completed in accordance with California *Education Code* 49162 and 49163 as notification of intent to
employ a minor. This form is also a Certificate of Age pursuant to California *Education Code* 49114.

(Print Information)

Minor's Information

Minor's Name *(First and Last)*	Home Phone	Grade
Home Address	City	Zip Code
Birth Date Social Security Number	Age	Student's Signature

School Information

School Name	School Phone
School Address	City Zip Code

To be filled in and signed by parent or legal guardian

*This minor is being employed at the place of work described with my full knowledge and consent. I hereby certify that to the best of
my knowledge and belief, the information herein is correct and true.*

Parent's Name *(Print First and Last)*	Parent's Signature	Date

To be filled in and signed by employer

Business Name or Agency of Placement	Business Phone	Supervisor's Name
Business Address	City	Zip Code

Employer's Maximum Expected Work Hours: _____ hours per day _____ hours per week

Describe nature of work to be performed: _____

*In compliance with California labor laws, this employee is covered by workers' compensation insurance. This business does not
discriminate unlawfully on the basis of race, ethnic background, religion, sex, sexual orientation, color, national origin, ancestry, age,
physical handicap, or medical condition. I hereby certify that, to the best of my knowledge, the information herein is correct and true.*

Employer's Name *(Print First and Last)*	Employer's Signature	Date

For authorized work permit issuer use ONLY

Maximum number of work hours when school is in session:								Maximum number of work hours when school is not in session:							
Mon	Tues	Wed	Thur	Fri	Sat	Sun	Total	Mon	Tues	Wed	Thur	Fri	Sat	Sun	Total

Proof of Minor's Age *(Evidence Type)*

Verifying Authority's Name and Title *(Print)*

Verifying Authority's Signature

Check Permit Type:

- [ ] Full-time
- [ ] Restricted
- [ ] General
- [ ] Work Experience Education, Vocational Education, or Personal Attendant
- [ ] Workability

For more information about child labor laws, contact the U.S. Department of Labor at http://www.dol.gov/, and the State of
California Department of Industrial Relations, Division of Labor Standards Enforcement at http://www.dir.ca.gov/DLSE/dlse.html.

Page 2 of Statement of Intent to Employ

CDE Form B1-1 (Rev. 08-13)

General Summary of Minors' Work Regulations

FLSA-Federal Labor Standards Act, CDE-California Department of Education, EC-California *Education Code*, LC-California *Labor Code*, CFR-California Federal Regulations, WEE-Work Experience Education, CVE-Cooperative Vocational Education

- If federal laws, state laws, and school district policies conflict, the more restrictive law (the one most protective of the minor) prevails (FLSA).

- Employers of minors required to attend school must sign a "Statement of Intent to Employ a Minor and Request for a Work Permit – Certificate of Age" (CDE Form B1-1) (*EC* 49162).

- Employers must retain a "Permit to Employ and Work" (CDE Form B1-4) for each employed minor *(EC* 49161).

- Work permits (CDE Form B1-4) must be retained for three years and be available for inspection by sanctioned authorities at all times (*EC* 49164).

- A work permit (CDE Form B1-4) must be revoked whenever the issuing authority determines the employment is illegal or is impairing the health or education of the minor (*EC* 49164).

- A day of rest from work is required in every seven days, and shall not exceed six days in seven (*LC* 551, 552).

Minors under the age of 18 may not work in environments declared hazardous or dangerous for young workers, examples listed below (*LC* 1294.1, 1294.5; 29 *CFR* 570 Subpart E):
1. Explosive exposure
2. Motor vehicle driving/outside helper
3. Roofing
4. Logging and sawmilling
5. Power-driven woodworking machines
6. Radiation exposure
7. Power-driven hoists/forklifts
8. Power-driven metal forming, punching, & shearing machines
9. Power saws and shears
10. Power-driving meat slicing/processing machines

HOURS OF WORK

16 & 17 Year Olds	14 & 15 Year Olds	12 & 13 Year Olds
Must have completed 7th grade to work while school is in session (*EC* 49112)	Must have completed 7th grade to work while school is in session (*EC* 49112)	Labor laws prohibit non-farm employment of children younger than 14. Special rules apply to agricultural work, domestic work in a private home, and the entertainment industry (*LC* 1285–1312)

Maximum Work Hours - School In Session

16 & 17 Year Olds	14 & 15 Year Olds	12 & 13 Year Olds
4 hours per day on any schoolday (*EC* 49112, 49116; *LC* 1391) 8 hours on any non-schoolday or on any day preceding a non-schoolday (*EC* 49112; *LC* 1391) 48 hours per week (*LC* 1391) WEE and CVE students & personal attendants may work more than 4 hours on a schoolday, but never more than 8 (*EC* 49116; *LC* 1391, 1392)	3 hours per schoolday outside of school hours (*EC* 49112, 49116; *LC* 1391) 8 hours on any non-schoolday 18 hours per week (*EC* 49116; *LC* 1391) WEE and CVE students may work during school hours and up to 23 hours per week (*EC* 49116; *LC* 1391)	2 hours per schoolday and a maximum of 4 hours per week (*EC* 49112)

Maximum Work Hours - School Not In Session

16 & 17 Year Olds	14 & 15 Year Olds	12 & 13 Year Olds
8 hours per day (*LC* 1391, 1392) 48 hours per week (*LC* 1391)	8 hours per day (*LC* 1391, 1392) 40 hours per week (*LC* 1391)	8 hours per day (*LC* 1391, 1392) 40 hours per week (*LC* 1391)

Spread of Hours

16 & 17 Year Olds	14 & 15 Year Olds	12 & 13 Year Olds
5 a.m.–10 p.m. However, until 12:30 a.m. on any evening preceding a non-schoolday (*LC* 1391) WEE and CVE students, with permission until 12:30 a.m. on any day (*LC* 1391.1) Messengers: 6 a.m.–9 p.m.	7 a.m.–7 p.m., except from June 1 through Labor Day, until 9 p.m. (*LC* 1391)	7 a.m.–7 p.m., except from June 1 through Labor Day, until 9 p.m. (*LC* 1391)

For more information about child labor laws, contact the U.S. Department of Labor at http://www.dol.gov/, and the State of California Department of Industrial Relations, Division of Labor Standards Enforcement at http://www.dir.ca.gov/DLSE/dlse.html.

◆ After you finish filling out the form, take it back to the school. The school will complete the last section.

◆ The school will then give you a work permit. You must take this permit to your employer. The permit must be put in your records before you can start work.

◆ You can start working now.

Here are two things you should know about your work permit:

◆ Work permits expire, and must be renewed if you are still a minor.

◆ Every time you get a new job, you must get a new work permit. Simply follow the same steps each time.

See SAMPLE Work Permits on the next two pages. The form may look different depending on where you live.

Sample Work Permit—1

State of Michigan: Combined Offer of Employment and Work Permit/Age Certificate
CA-7 for minors 16 and 17 years of age

Permit Number for School Use
(optional)

Employer Information:
- The employer must have a completed front and back yellow work permit form on file **before** a minor begins work.
- The employer or an employee who is 18 years of age or older must provide competent adult supervision at all times.
- The employer of the minor must comply with federal, state, and local laws and regulations including nondiscrimination against any
  applicant or employee because of race, color, religion, national origin or ancestry, age, gender, height, weight, marital status, or disability.
- The employer must return the work permit to the issuing officer upon termination of the minor's employment.

Directions: Please type or print using black ink pen. ALL FIELDS MUST BE COMPLETED. Back of this form must have summary of requirements.

Section I: Each Box must be Completed by Minor Applicant and Parent/Guardian

Name of Minor: Address: City & ZIP:

Age: Date of Birth (MM/DD/YYYY):   Last 4 Digits of Soc. Number   Contact Number:

Name of School (present or last attended):   School Address: City & ZIP:

Last Grade Completed: School Status (check one):   Type of Business (i.e., fast food, manufacturing):
    □ in school, □ home school, □ online/cyber/virtual school, □ not attending school

Signature of Minor   □ Parent/ □ Guardian Name (check one):   Parent/Guardian Telephone:

Section II: Each Box must be Completed by the Employer - Offer of Employment

Name of Business: Address: City & ZIP:

Earliest Start Time Not before   Latest End Time Not later   Hours per Day   Days per Week: Total Hours of Employment:
3:00 pm (Monday-Friday)   10:30 pm (Sunday-Thursday)   No more than 24 when school is in session
When school is in session   11:30 pm (Friday-Saturday)   No More than 8   No more than 6   No more than 48 when school is not in session
No earlier than 6:00 am (Sat-Sun)   11:30 pm school vacation   Spring/Summer/Christmas/Winter vacation

Applicants Job Title: Hourly Wage: Name of Job Duties/Tasks to be Performed by the Minor: Name Equipment/Tools to be Used by Minor:

Individual Application for Hours Deviation for 16 and 17 Year Old Minors along with this original yellow CA-7 must be mail to:
MDE/OCTE P.O. Box 30712, Lansing, Michigan, 48909, for approval.

Signature of Employer: Title: Telephone: Date:

Section III: Certification
Each Box must be Completed by a Michigan School's Issuing Officer – Must be Signed by the Issuing Officer to be Valid

This is to certify that: (1) the minor personally appeared before me, (2) this form was properly completed, (3) listed job duties are in compliance with state and federal
laws and regulations, (4) listed hours are in compliance with state and federal laws and regulations, (5) this form was signed by student and employer, and I authorize
the issuance of this work permit.

Evidence of Age confirmed by (Issuing officer checks one):

□ Birth Certificate, □ Driver's License, □ School Record, □ Certificate of Arrival in U.S □ Hospital Record of Birth, □ Baptismal Certificate,
□ Other (Describe):

Number of Work Hours per week, when School is in Session: Number of Work Hours while school is not in session (Summer, Spring, Xmas vacation)
    No more than 24 per week   No More than 48 per week

Name of School District: Address: City, State, and ZIP: Telephone:

Signature of Issuing Officer: Title: Printed Name of Issuing Officer: Issue Date:

Form CA-7 (revised 02/07/2017) Combined Offer of Employment & Work Permit and Age Certificate   **Must Print front and back on Yellow Paper.**
Instructions for completing CA-7 must be printed on back of form to be valid.
Must submit original yellow front and back CA-7 when submitting Individual Application for Hours Deviation form.

Sample Work Permit—2

AT-17
Rev. 5/10

THIS APPLICATION DOES NOT AUTHORIZE EMPLOYMENT

THE UNIVERSITY OF THE STATE OF NEW YORK
THE STATE EDUCATION DEPARTMENT
ALBANY, NY 12234
APPLICATION FOR EMPLOYMENT CERTIFICATE
See reverse side of this form for information concerning employment of minors.
All signatures must be handwritten in ink, and applicant must appear in person before the certifying official.

PART I – Parental Consent – (To be completed by applicant and parent or guardian)
Parent or guardian must appear at the school or issuing center to sign the application for the first certificate for full-time employment, unless the minor is a graduate of a four-year high school and presents evidence thereof. For all other certificates, the parent or guardian must sign the application, but need not appear in person to do so.

Date........................

I, ... Age ....
　　　[Applicant]

Home Address ...., apply for a certificate as checked below
　　　[Full Home Address including Zip Code]

☐　　Nonfactory Employment Certificate – Valid for lawful employment of a minor 14 or 15 years of age enrolled in day school when attendance is not required.

☐　　Student General Employment Certificate – Valid for lawful employment of a minor 16 or 17 years of age enrolled in day school when attendance is not required.

☐　　Full-Time Employment Certificate – Valid for lawful employment of a minor 16 or 17 years of age who is not attending day school.

I hereby consent to the required examination and employment certification as indicated above.

....
[Signature of Parent or Guardian]

PART II – Evidence of Age – (To be completed by issuing official only)
.... – Check evidence of age accepted – Document # (if any) ....
　　　[Date of Birth]

Birth Certificate　　State Issued Photo　　I.D Driver's License　　Schooling Record　　Other...................
　　[Specify]

PART III – Certificate of Physical Fitness
Applicant shall present documentation of physical exam from a school or private physician, physician's assistant or nurse practitioner licensed to practice within New York State. Said examination must have been given within 12 months prior to issuance of the employment certificate. Date of physical exam on file with school .... If physical exam is over 12 months, provide student with certificate of physical fitness to be completed by school medical director or private health care provider.
If the physical exam or Certificate of Physical Fitness is limited with regards to allowed work/activity, the issuing official shall issue a Limited Employment Certificate (valid for a period not to exceed 6 months unless the limitation noted by the physician is permanent, then the certificate will remain valid until the minor changes jobs. Enter the limitation on the employment certificate. THE PHYSICIAN'S CERTIFICATION SHOULD BE RETURNED TO THE APPLICANT.

PART IV – Pledge of Employment – (To be completed by prospective employer)
Part IV must be completed only for: (a) a minor with a medical limitation; and (b) for a minor 16 years of age or legally able to withdraw from school, according to Section 3205 of the Education Law, and must show proof of having a job.
The undersigned will employ .... residing at ....
　　　　　　　　　　　　　　　　　　　　　　[Applicant]

as .... at ....
　　　[Description of Applicant's Work]　　　　　　　　　　[Job Location]

for .... days per week .... hours per day, beginning .... a.m. .... p.m.

....　Factory　　ending............................... a.m. .... p.m.
　　　[Name of Firm]

　　　　　　　　　　　　　　　　　　Nonfactory　　..
　　　　　　　　　　　　　　　　　　　　　　　　　　　　　　　　　[Address of Firm]

....　Starting date ....　..
　　　[Telephone Number]　　　　　　　　　　　　　　　　　　　　　[Signature of Employer]

PART V – Schooling Record – (To be completed by school official)
Part V must be completed only for a minor 16 years of age who is leaving school and resides in a district (New York City and Buffalo) which require a minor 16 years of age to attend school, according to Section 3205 of the Education Law.

I certify that the records of ....　...
　　　　　　　　　　　　　[Name of School]　　　　　　　　　　　[Address]

Show that .... whose date of birth is ....
　　　　[Name of Applicant]

Is in grade..　..
　　　　　　　　　　　　　　　　　　　　　　　[Signature of Principal or Designee]

PART VI – Employment Certification – (To be completed by issuing official only)
Certificate Number ....　Date Issued ....

....　...　...
[School or Issuing Center]　　　　　[Address]　　　　　　　[Signature of Issuing Officer]

FORM I-9: Employment Eligibility Verification

The Employment Eligibility Verification form, also called Form I-9, is also a government form. Everyone who works must fill it out. It proves that a new employee has the right to work in the United States of America.

Your employer will give the form to you. Both you and your employer must fill it out. It must be completed at the time of hire.

To work in the United States of America (USA), you must be one of the following:
- ☐ A citizen or national of the USA
- ☐ A lawful permanent resident
- ☐ An alien authorized to work in the USA

The employer will ask you to provide certain documents required by the Form I-9. For instance, you will need to provide one or two different forms of identification. Here are some examples of acceptable forms:

- ◆ Driver's License
- ◆ Social Security Card
- ◆ State-issued ID Card
- ◆ School Record
- ◆ Report Card
- ◆ Hospital Birth Record

You must bring the required ID within three business days of the date your new job begins. Do not bring photocopies of your documents: bring <u>original documents</u> only.

Page 1 of Form I-9

Employment Eligibility Verification
Department of Homeland Security
U.S. Citizenship and Immigration Services

Form I-9 Instructions

Section 1: Employee information and attestation: Your employee is responsible for completing this section. As part of this, they will indicate their current immigration status such as a citizen of the U.S., non-citizen national of the U.S., lawful permanent resident, or alien authorized to work in the U.S.

This part of the form should be filled out no later than the employee's first day of employment. A Preparer and/or Translator Certification section will also need to be completed and signed if a translator was used to assist the employee with filling out the form or translating the information in any form.

Section 2: Employer review and verification: Within three days of starting work, the newly hired employee must present specific documents attesting to their chosen status. Employees can present one selection from List A, or one selection from List B **and** one selection from List C below.

Here is a partial list of acceptable documents. The I-9 instruction form contains a more detailed list.

LIST A	LIST B	LIST C
U.S. Passport	U.S. Driver's License	Social Security Card
U.S. Passport Card	U.S. State I.D. Card	Birth Certificate
Permanent Resident Card	Voter Registration Card	U.S. Citizen I.D. Card
Foreign Passport w/I-551	U.S. Military Card	Receipt for application to replace Social Security Card

Page 2 of Form I-9

 Employment Eligibility Verification
Department of Homeland Security
U.S. Citizenship and Immigration Services

USCIS
Form I-9
OMB No. 1615-0047
Expires 08/31/2019

▶**START HERE:** Read instructions carefully before completing this form. The instructions must be available, either in paper or electronically, during completion of this form. Employers are liable for errors in the completion of this form.

ANTI-DISCRIMINATION NOTICE: It is illegal to discriminate against work-authorized individuals. Employers **CANNOT** specify which document(s) an employee may present to establish employment authorization and identity. The refusal to hire or continue to employ an individual because the documentation presented has a future expiration date may also constitute illegal discrimination.

Section 1. Employee Information and Attestation *(Employees must complete and sign Section 1 of Form I-9 no later than the first day of employment, but not before accepting a job offer.)*

Last Name *(Family Name)*	First Name *(Given Name)*	Middle Initial	Other Last Names Used *(if any)*
Address *(Street Number and Name)*	Apt. Number	City or Town	State	ZIP Code
Date of Birth *(mm/dd/yyyy)*	U.S. Social Security Number	Employee's E-mail Address	Employee's Telephone Number

I am aware that federal law provides for imprisonment and/or fines for false statements or use of false documents in connection with the completion of this form.

I attest, under penalty of perjury, that I am (check one of the following boxes):

☐ 1. A citizen of the United States

☐ 2. A noncitizen national of the United States *(See instructions)*

☐ 3. A lawful permanent resident   (Alien Registration Number/USCIS Number): _____

☐ 4. An alien authorized to work   until (expiration date, if applicable, mm/dd/yyyy): _____
    Some aliens may write "N/A" in the expiration date field. *(See instructions)*

Aliens authorized to work must provide only one of the following document numbers to complete Form I-9:
An Alien Registration Number/USCIS Number OR Form I-94 Admission Number OR Foreign Passport Number.

1. Alien Registration Number/USCIS Number: _____
    OR
2. Form I-94 Admission Number: _____
    OR
3. Foreign Passport Number: _____
    Country of Issuance: _____

QR Code - Section 1
Do Not Write In This Space

Signature of Employee	Today's Date *(mm/dd/yyyy)*

Preparer and/or Translator Certification (check one):
☐ I did not use a preparer or translator   ☐ A preparer(s) and/or translator(s) assisted the employee in completing Section 1.
(Fields below must be completed and signed when preparers and/or translators assist an employee in completing Section 1.)

I attest, under penalty of perjury, that I have assisted in the completion of Section 1 of this form and that to the best of my knowledge the information is true and correct.

Signature of Preparer or Translator	Today's Date *(mm/dd/yyyy)*
Last Name *(Family Name)*	First Name *(Given Name)*
Address *(Street Number and Name)*	City or Town	State	ZIP Code

  *Employer Completes Next Page* 🛑

Form I-9 07/17/17 N   Page 1 of 3

Page 3 of Form I-9

LISTS OF ACCEPTABLE DOCUMENTS
All documents must be UNEXPIRED

Employees may present one selection from List A
or a combination of one selection from List B and one selection from List C.

LIST A Documents that Establish Both Identity and Employment Authorization		LIST B Documents that Establish Identity	LIST C Documents that Establish Employment Authorization
	OR	AND	
1. U.S. Passport or U.S. Passport Card		1. Driver's license or ID card issued by a State or outlying possession of the United States provided it contains a photograph or information such as name, date of birth, gender, height, eye color, and address	1. A Social Security Account Number card, unless the card includes one of the following restrictions: (1) NOT VALID FOR EMPLOYMENT (2) VALID FOR WORK ONLY WITH INS AUTHORIZATION (3) VALID FOR WORK ONLY WITH DHS AUTHORIZATION
2. Permanent Resident Card or Alien Registration Receipt Card (Form I-551)			
3. Foreign passport that contains a temporary I-551 stamp or temporary I-551 printed notation on a machine-readable immigrant visa		2. ID card issued by federal, state or local government agencies or entities, provided it contains a photograph or information such as name, date of birth, gender, height, eye color, and address	
4. Employment Authorization Document that contains a photograph (Form I-766)			2. Certification of report of birth issued by the Department of State (Forms DS-1350, FS-545, FS-240)
		3. School ID card with a photograph	
5. For a nonimmigrant alien authorized to work for a specific employer because of his or her status: a. Foreign passport; and b. Form I-94 or Form I-94A that has the following: (1) The same name as the passport; and (2) An endorsement of the alien's nonimmigrant status as long as that period of endorsement has not yet expired and the proposed employment is not in conflict with any restrictions or limitations identified on the form.		4. Voter's registration card	3. Original or certified copy of birth certificate issued by a State, county, municipal authority, or territory of the United States bearing an official seal
		5. U.S. Military card or draft record	
		6. Military dependent's ID card	
		7. U.S. Coast Guard Merchant Mariner Card	4. Native American tribal document
			5. U.S. Citizen ID Card (Form I-197)
		8. Native American tribal document	6. Identification Card for Use of Resident Citizen in the United States (Form I-179)
		9. Driver's license issued by a Canadian government authority	
		For persons under age 18 who are unable to present a document listed above:	7. Employment authorization document issued by the Department of Homeland Security
6. Passport from the Federated States of Micronesia (FSM) or the Republic of the Marshall Islands (RMI) with Form I-94 or Form I-94A indicating nonimmigrant admission under the Compact of Free Association Between the United States and the FSM or RMI		10. School record or report card	
		11. Clinic, doctor, or hospital record	
		12. Day-care or nursery school record	

Examples of many of these documents appear in Part 13 of the Handbook for Employers (M-274).

Refer to the instructions for more information about acceptable receipts.

Form W-4

Form W-4 is a government tax form. The purpose of this form is to tell the employer how much tax (money) to take from your paycheck each time you are paid. Most of the time, the form is filled out on the day that you are hired. The government says that everyone must complete the W-4 form and report how much money they have been paid. The amount of money taken from your paycheck will be based on what you write on the W-4 form.

Your employer can help you fill out the form. However, before completing your form, be sure to ask your parents or legal guardians if they put you on their W-4 as a dependent. If you are claimed as a dependent, this may change the information that you write on your W-4.

Page 1 of Form W-4

Form W-4

Department of the Treasury
Internal Revenue Service

Employee's Withholding Certificate

▶ Complete Form W-4 so that your employer can withhold the correct federal income tax from your pay.
▶ Give Form W-4 to your employer.
▶ Your withholding is subject to review by the IRS.

OMB No. 1545-0074

2020

Step 1: Enter Personal Information	(a) First name and middle initial	Last name	(b) Social security number
	Address		▶ Does your name match the name on your social security card? If not, to ensure you get credit for your earnings, contact SSA at 800-772-1213 or go to www.ssa.gov.
	City or town, state, and ZIP code		

(c) ☐ Single or Married filing separately
☐ Married filing jointly (or Qualifying widow(er))
☐ Head of household (Check only if you're unmarried and pay more than half the costs of keeping up a home for yourself and a qualifying individual.)

Complete Steps 2–4 ONLY if they apply to you; otherwise, skip to Step 5. See page 2 for more information on each step, who can claim exemption from withholding, when to use the online estimator, and privacy.

Step 2:
Multiple Jobs or Spouse Works

Complete this step if you (1) hold more than one job at a time, or (2) are married filing jointly and your spouse also works. The correct amount of withholding depends on income earned from all of these jobs.

Do **only one** of the following.

(a) Use the estimator at *www.irs.gov/W4App* for most accurate withholding for this step (and Steps 3–4); **or**

(b) Use the Multiple Jobs Worksheet on page 3 and enter the result in Step 4(c) below for roughly accurate withholding; **or**

(c) If there are only two jobs total, you may check this box. Do the same on Form W-4 for the other job. This option is accurate for jobs with similar pay; otherwise, more tax than necessary may be withheld . . . . . ▶ ☐

TIP: To be accurate, submit a 2020 Form W-4 for all other jobs. If you (or your spouse) have self-employment income, including as an independent contractor, use the estimator.

Complete Steps 3–4(b) on Form W-4 for only ONE of these jobs. Leave those steps blank for the other jobs. (Your withholding will be most accurate if you complete Steps 3–4(b) on the Form W-4 for the highest paying job.)

Step 3: Claim Dependents	If your income will be $200,000 or less ($400,000 or less if married filing jointly):		
	Multiply the number of qualifying children under age 17 by $2,000 ▶ $		
	Multiply the number of other dependents by $500 . . . . ▶ $		
	Add the amounts above and enter the total here	3	$

Step 4 (optional): Other Adjustments	(a) **Other income (not from jobs).** If you want tax withheld for other income you expect this year that won't have withholding, enter the amount of other income here. This may include interest, dividends, and retirement income	4(a)	$
	(b) **Deductions.** If you expect to claim deductions other than the standard deduction and want to reduce your withholding, use the Deductions Worksheet on page 3 and enter the result here	4(b)	$
	(c) **Extra withholding.** Enter any additional tax you want withheld each **pay period** .	4(c)	$

Step 5: Sign Here	Under penalties of perjury, I declare that this certificate, to the best of my knowledge and belief, is true, correct, and complete.	
	▶ _____ Employee's signature (This form is not valid unless you sign it.)	▶ _____ Date

Employers Only	Employer's name and address	First date of employment	Employer identification number (EIN)

For Privacy Act and Paperwork Reduction Act Notice, see page 3.　　Cat. No. 10220Q　　Form **W-4** (2020)

Page 2 Form W-4

General Instructions

Future Developments

For the latest information about developments related to Form W-4, such as legislation enacted after it was published, go to *www.irs.gov/FormW4*.

Purpose of Form

Complete Form W-4 so that your employer can withhold the correct federal income tax from your pay. If too little is withheld, you will generally owe tax when you file your tax return and may owe a penalty. If too much is withheld, you will generally be due a refund. Complete a new Form W-4 when changes to your personal or financial situation would change the entries on the form. For more information on withholding and when you must furnish a new Form W-4, see Pub. 505.

Exemption from withholding. You may claim exemption from withholding for 2020 if you meet both of the following conditions: you had no federal income tax liability in 2019 **and** you expect to have no federal income tax liability in 2020. You had no federal income tax liability in 2019 if (1) your total tax on line 16 on your 2019 Form 1040 or 1040-SR is zero (or less than the sum of lines 18a, 18b, and 18c), or (2) you were not required to file a return because your income was below the filing threshold for your correct filing status. If you claim exemption, you will have no income tax withheld from your paycheck and may owe taxes and penalties when you file your 2020 tax return. To claim exemption from withholding, certify that you meet both of the conditions above by writing "Exempt" on Form W-4 in the space below Step 4(c). Then, complete Steps 1(a), 1(b), and 5. Do not complete any other steps. You will need to submit a new Form W-4 by February 16, 2021.

Your privacy. If you prefer to limit information provided in Steps 2 through 4, use the online estimator, which will also increase accuracy.

As an alternative to the estimator: if you have concerns with Step 2(c), you may choose Step 2(b); if you have concerns with Step 4(a), you may enter an additional amount you want withheld per pay period in Step 4(c). If this is the only job in your household, you may instead check the box in Step 2(c), which will increase your withholding and significantly reduce your paycheck (often by thousands of dollars over the year).

When to use the estimator. Consider using the estimator at *www.irs.gov/W4App* if you:

1. Expect to work only part of the year;

2. Have dividend or capital gain income, or are subject to additional taxes, such as the additional Medicare tax;

3. Have self-employment income (see below); or

4. Prefer the most accurate withholding for multiple job situations.

Self-employment. Generally, you will owe both income and self-employment taxes on any self-employment income you receive separate from the wages you receive as an employee. If you want to pay these taxes through withholding from your wages, use the estimator at *www.irs.gov/W4App* to figure the amount to have withheld.

Nonresident alien. If you're a nonresident alien, see Notice 1392, Supplemental Form W-4 Instructions for Nonresident Aliens, before completing this form.

Specific Instructions

Step 1(c). Check your anticipated filing status. This will determine the standard deduction and tax rates used to compute your withholding.

Step 2. Use this step if you (1) have more than one job at the same time, or (2) are married filing jointly and you and your spouse both work.

Option **(a)** most accurately calculates the additional tax you need to have withheld, while option **(b)** does so with a little less accuracy.

If you (and your spouse) have a total of only two jobs, you may instead check the box in option **(c)**. The box must also be checked on the Form W-4 for the other job. If the box is checked, the standard deduction and tax brackets will be cut in half for each job to calculate withholding. This option is roughly accurate for jobs with similar pay; otherwise, more tax than necessary may be withheld, and this extra amount will be larger the greater the difference in pay is between the two jobs.

 Multiple jobs. Complete Steps 3 through 4(b) on only one Form W-4. Withholding will be most accurate if you do this on the Form W-4 for the highest paying job.

Step 3. Step 3 of Form W-4 provides instructions for determining the amount of the child tax credit and the credit for other dependents that you may be able to claim when you file your tax return. To qualify for the child tax credit, the child must be under age 17 as of December 31, must be your dependent who generally lives with you for more than half the year, and must have the required social security number. You may be able to claim a credit for other dependents for whom a child tax credit can't be claimed, such as an older child or a qualifying relative. For additional eligibility requirements for these credits, see Pub. 972, Child Tax Credit and Credit for Other Dependents. You can also include **other tax credits** in this step, such as education tax credits and the foreign tax credit. To do so, add an estimate of the amount for the year to your credits for dependents and enter the total amount in Step 3. Including these credits will increase your paycheck and reduce the amount of any refund you may receive when you file your tax return.

Step 4 (optional).

Step 4(a). Enter in this step the total of your other estimated income for the year, if any. You shouldn't include income from any jobs or self-employment. If you complete Step 4(a), you likely won't have to make estimated tax payments for that income. If you prefer to pay estimated tax rather than having tax on other income withheld from your paycheck, see Form 1040-ES, Estimated Tax for Individuals.

Step 4(b). Enter in this step the amount from the Deductions Worksheet, line 5, if you expect to claim deductions other than the basic standard deduction on your 2020 tax return and want to reduce your withholding to account for these deductions. This includes both itemized deductions and other deductions such as for student loan interest and IRAs.

Step 4(c). Enter in this step any additional tax you want withheld from your pay **each pay period**, including any amounts from the Multiple Jobs Worksheet, line 4. Entering an amount here will reduce your paycheck and will either increase your refund or reduce any amount of tax that you owe.

Step 10 → Review

Please complete the following quiz.

1. In most cases, you must be at least 14 years of age to get a work permit.

    ☐ True ☐ False

2. People under the age of 17 can work as a fire fighter if they want to.

    ☐ True ☐ False

3. Once you get a work permit, you can work as many hours per day as you want to, just as long if you finish your homework.

    ☐ True ☐ False

4. Only students can get a work permit.

    ☐ True ☐ False

5. The employer will give you a work permit.

    ☐ True ☐ False

6. You need to get a new work permit every time you get a new job.

    ☐ True ☐ False

7. Work permits never expire.

    ☐ True ☐ False

8. Only students have to fill out Form I-9.

    ☐ True ☐ False

9. Form I-9 is used to prove that you have the right to work in the United States of America.

    ☐ True ☐ False

10. You will get the Form I-9 from your employer.

    ☐ True ☐ False

11. Form I-9 is filled out when you quit your job.

    ☐ True ☐ False

12. Your school will fill out the Form I-9 for you.

    ☐ True ☐ False

13. You fill out a Form I-9 so that your employer can take the right amount of taxes from your paycheck.

    ☐ True ☐ False

14. Both you and your employer must fill out the Form I-9.

    ☐ True ☐ False

15. You don't have to fill out a Form W-4 if you don't want to.

    ☐ True ☐ False

16. You fill out a Form W-4 so that your employer can take the right amount of taxes from your paycheck.

    ☐ True ☐ False

17. People under the age of 18 don't have to complete Form W-4.

    ☐ True ☐ False

18. It does not matter what you write on Form W-4, employers will know how much tax to take out of your paycheck.

    ☐ True ☐ False

19. The employer will wait 30 days before asking you to fill out Form W-4.

☐ True   ☐ False

20. Form W-4 is a government form.
☐ True   ☐ False

Step 10 → Answers

1. True

2. False

3. False

4. True

5. False

6. True

7. False

8. False

9. True

10. True

11. False

12. False

13. False

14. True

15. False

16. True

17. False

18. False

19. False

20. True

Bonus Step: → Dos & Don'ts Now That You Have a Job!

Once you get a job, you need to know how to keep it! The DOS and DON'TS discussed here can help you. Nobody wants to get fired from a job. Not only is it embarrassing, it looks bad on your employment record. So, pay special attention to these helpful tips:

◆ DO try to arrive at work 5 to 10 minutes before you are due to start on your first day.

◆ DO find out where you should go and who you should see on your first day of work.

◆ DO find out your supervisor's name and what job he or she does.

◆ DO make sure that you have your company's phone number.

◆ DO report to work on time every day and be sure to find out about the company's policies (rules) about coming to work late or too early.

◆ DON'T have your parent or legal guardian call if you're going to be absent! The employer wants to hear from you personally.

◆ DO show respect for all managers or supervisors at your job. Even supervisors who are not directly in charge of you have more authority than you do and can make problems for you.

  o Note: It is a good idea to have respect for everyone. If you treat others with respect, they are more likely to show respect for you!

◆ DON'T let your friends or family call you at work or visit you unless there is something wrong. Employers don't like for you to get personal calls, and don't like family or friends "hanging out" at their business.

◆ DO find out your company's policy about phone calls and visitors. Make sure you also learn any rules about receiving and making personal phone calls.

◆ DO try to be a good employee by following company rules.

◆ DON'T chew gum, eat, or talk loudly in the work area.

◆ DO smile and be friendly to customers if you have a job working face to face with them.

◆ DON'T be "mean" to anyone! A good rule to follow is to treat others the way you want to be treated.

◆ DO try to be friendly while at work. It makes your job, and everyone else's, a lot easier to handle.

◆ DO give your work number to your parents or the people you live with in case any problems come up.

◆ DON'T quit your job without giving one or two weeks' notice (warning). If you tell your employer that you are quitting a week or two before you plan to leave, there will be time to find someone to take your place.

TIP: Once you find a job, be sure to learn all that you can and do your best to become a good employee. Remember, most of us will work for many years, so it makes sense to make it an enjoyable journey.

Bonus Step → Review

Read the following questions and choose the correct answers.

1. If you are going to be late or absent from work, who should call your employer?

    a. A friend
    b. You
    c. Your teacher
    d. Your parent or guardian
    e. No one

2. What kind of employee should you be at work?

    a. A good employee who follows company rules.
    b. A funny employee who laughs and tells jokes.
    c. An employee who chews gum, eats, and talks loudly while working.
    d. It doesn't matter what kind of employee you are.

3. If you want to quit your job, how much notice (warning) should you give?

    a. None
    b. One day
    c. One or two weeks
    d. One hour

4. How should you treat a supervisor at your job who is not "your" supervisor?

    a. Treat them unkindly.
    b. Act like you don't care who they are.
    c. Treat them like you would any other employee.
    d. Treat them with respect.

5. What should you do about friends or family calling and visiting you at work?

    a. Tell your friends and family it is okay to call you at work.
    b. Tell them that it is all right to visit, but not to call.
    c. Tell your family and friends about the company rules.
    d. Nothing—they will figure it out for themselves.

Bonus Step → Answers

1. b

2. a

3. c

4. d

5. c

Glossary

Agreement: A written or spoken understanding between two or more people.

Attitude: A way of thinking: how or what one thinks about something and how they show those feelings.

Claim: (Legal) To provide for.

Community: Neighborhood. Where people live.

Dependent: One who is taken care of by someone else.

Discriminate: To make distinctions on the basis of class, race, religion, etc., without regard to individual merit; to show preference or prejudice toward certain people.

DOB: Date of Birth

Document: A piece of paper that gives information, instructions, or facts.

Employment Development Department (EDD): A government agency that works with many different employers. Their main function is to help job hunters find work. There are many locations throughout the state and Internet access is also available.

ExtraCurricular: Activities offered on an after-school basis entirely and provide no grade or credit toward graduation (i.e., sports teams, cheerleaders, marching band).

Expire: To end.

Foreign: Of or from a place or country other than the one being considered.

Guardian: One who has the legal right to take care of someone under the age of 18.

Human Resources (HR): The department in a company that is responsible for hiring new employees. They manage the payroll, benefits, retirement, and company polices. It is also referred to as the HR department.

Letter of Recommendation: A letter that makes a statement of support for someone, for example, a job candidate. In most cases, the letter should consist of three or four paragraphs and not be over one page in length.

Parental: Relates to parents.

Policy: Rules, guidelines, procedures.

Position: Rank, job, title.

Provisions: Requirements. To supply what is needed.

Punctuation: The use of special marks to make writing more clear. Examples of these marks are commas, colons, periods, etc.

References: Providing the name of a person who knows of your personal strengths and positive behavior and qualities. For example, that you are honest, trustworthy, dependable, creative, etc.

Regulations: Rules, guidelines, set of laws, policy.

Renew: To begin again, to get a new one.

Respect: To hold in high regard.

Résumé* (pronounced rez-oo-mey): A written summary about your skills, abilities, and work experience. It is usually one page long, and requested by most employers.

Solely: Only, alone, exclusively.

Supervisor: Boss, one in charge of someone or something.

Unconventional: Not conforming to accepted standards.

Congratulations on completing our easy-to-read guide!

The information here is only the beginning of your employment journey. Remember to find work that you love, and you will always enjoy the journey.

Good Luck!

Printed in the United States
By Bookmasters